Tricky Spellings
in Cartoons for Children

Tricky Spellings in Cartoons for Children

Lidia Stanton

Jessica Kingsley Publishers
London and Philadelphia

First published in Great Britain in 2021 by Jessica Kingsley Publishers
An Hachette Company

1

Copyright © Lidia Stanton 2021

Front cover image source: Sophie Kennedy.

A CIP catalogue record for this title is available from the
British Library and the Library of Congress

ISBN 978 1 78775 632 8
eISBN 978 1 78775 633 5

Printed and bound in China by Leo Paper Products Ltd.

Jessica Kingsley Publishers' policy is to use papers that are natural,
renewable, and recyclable products and made from wood grown in
sustainable forests. The logging and manufacturing processes are expected
to conform to the environmental regulations of the country of origin.

Jessica Kingsley Publishers
Carmelite House
50 Victoria Embankment
London EC4Y 0DZ

www.jkp.com

Contents

Introduction

Following the success of *200 Tricky Spellings in Cartoons* in the UK, I was asked by parents and teachers to produce a similar resource for children of elementary school age in the US. Enthusiastically, I set about collecting a new set of tricky words. And here it is—a compilation of over 160 hints for 264 new spellings with color illustrations.

Is this book for my child?

This book is not a structured spelling program. It does not replace any part of a child's current literacy instruction at school. It complements it to help equip them with additional ways to remember tricky spellings.

It's suitable for children who:

- prefer to learn by seeing and doing
- have tried traditional spelling strategies (e.g. "Look, Cover, Write, Check" and breaking words into sounds and syllables) but with limited success
- continue to confuse similar sounding and similar looking words
- have dyslexia or other specific learning disabilities.

How mnemonics work

About 30 percent of English words can't be spelled using phonics. Their spelling patterns have to be memorized. Children might initially spell *what* as *wot* and *eight* as *eit* or *ate*. But if we help them identify patterns within words, for example break *what* into *w* (the first sound) and a phonetically regular word *hat* (w + hat), the spelling becomes easier to recall. In order to consolidate memory for the new spelling, why not act it out with the child: *What? A hat? What hat? Oh, I've got one*

11

on my head... How did it end up there? What? The wind blew it over? While many kindergarten and first grade children will learn tricky spellings using traditional methods with no trouble, some will continue misspelling them beyond grade 5 and 6—these children may benefit from the helping hand of mnemonics.

Mnemonics (pronounced with a silent front letter *m* [ni'monics]) are memory triggers that help us remember things we easily forget, for example telephone numbers, left/right directions, and tricky words. Children and adults enjoy using mnemonics because of their funny and unusual associations with things. They provide humor that often helps learning and supports long-term memory. What's more, mnemonics require almost no effort to learn.

About the mnemonics in this book

Most mnemonics in this publication are in the public domain—they are widely used by teachers, parents, and grandparents, and people with dyslexia. They are shared and handed down from one generation to another. Stylistic variations exist but the underlying ideas have remained unchanged for years. For this reason, it is virtually impossible to trace the exact origin of a particular mnemonic in order to accurately reference it.

Many spelling hints in this book are suggestions I received from readers who contacted me after they'd enjoyed *200 Tricky Spellings in Cartoons*: elementary school teachers, teaching assistants, dyslexia practitioners, and parents. I am very grateful for all the fantastic ideas, which I successfully use in my own dyslexia support practice.

This book doesn't contain every tricky spelling a child will encounter in elementary school, only some of the most common ones. As I continue receiving suggestions from educators and parents, there will be a part two to this publication that will make the spelling mnemonics bank more complete, if that is ever possible.

How to use this book

Help the child find the tricky word in the index at the back of the book. Read the short text together and ensure the child's understanding of the spelling hint. Don't forget to have fun exploring the visual hints and story lines. Talk about similar familiar situations so the child can relate to the idea. Help them turn their experiences into a new funny or silly story that links directly to the mnemonic. Mnemonics work best when they are personal.

It's important to refer back to the newly learned mnemonic later the same day and in the following days using fun activities that will ensure memory consolidation. Focus on action and play while combining as many senses as possible during learning: use pretend play to act out stories and situations, encourage visualization, and experiment with fun voices. Always focus on the "tricky" part of the word: *How did you remember it?* Below are suggestions you might find useful.

Ask the child to write the word:

- on the refrigerator, windows, and glass sliding doors using a wipeable marker (make a rule that no other markers are allowed to avoid permanent damage)
- on the sidewalk using colored chalk
- on the ground or fence using a squirty water bottle
- in shaving cream on the table, or spread the shaving cream on the surface so the child can use their finger to write the word
- in a baking tray filled with a shallow layer of salt or flour using their finger or a wooden spoon.

Help the child to:

- mold the word out of putty or dough
- make the word out of small building blocks
- bake the letters out of pastry or cookie dough, arrange them in the right order, and then enjoy eating the word.

Encourage the child to:

- recall the spelling mnemonic while bouncing on a trampoline or sofa (if allowed)
- say the tricky part of the word in a funny voice, a different accent, or a singing voice
- draw a picture/make a poster with the word and display at home or school.

The best way to learn is to teach: ask the child to teach tricky spellings to other family members and their friends.

I hope you will have lots of fun!

Lidia Stanton

1
Early
High-Frequency
Words

what
what hat?

w**hen**
hen

W**hen** did you get up, **hen**?

As early as the cows.

W**hen** will you go to bed,   **hen**?

I'm so tired, about now.

who
wicked hairy ogre

why
why hate yogurt?

here
where
there

Here
every
rainbow
ends

Where?
here

There?

Not there. Here.
See? Where the gold is.
My gold!

The word "here" hides inside "where" and "there."

how
on wheels

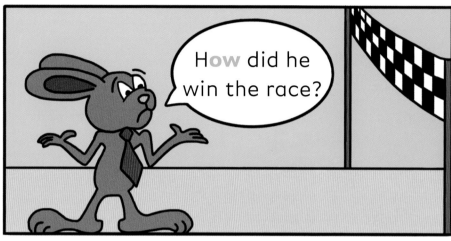

Did someone say sausages? Yum!

But what about Dad? **Does** he like them?

No, **D**ad **o**nly **e**ats **s**andwiches.

does

does Oliver eat sausages?

Oliver is 5 today. Next week I will be 10.

I need something that I like
to give to my good friend.

I wonder... does Oliver eat sausages?

one

only **on**e?

Only **on**e sausage for me?

Only **on**e star for my picture?

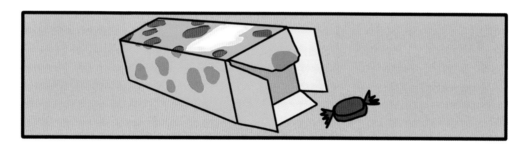

Only **on**e left?

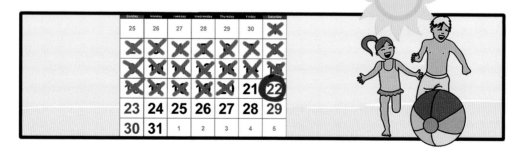

Yay! **On**ly **on**e day till the vacation!

Mr. and Mrs.
Mr. Red and Mrs. Red Socks

Mr. Red was like no other man; he was red.

But his wife had no color when they wed.

"My dear wife, here's a present in a box."

And that's how she became Mrs. Red Socks.

w**ant**

ant

I want an **ant**.

You can't snack all day.

I don't w**ant** to eat.

I w**ant** to play!

said
Who said dancing is silly?

Snakes and insects dance.

Sally Ann is dancing.

Smart Alec is dancing.

And I dance!

because

Not many people know that

big **e**lephants **c**an't **a**lways **u**se **s**mall **e**xits,

and that

big **e**lephants **c**an't **a**dd **u**p **s**ums **e**asily,

but everyone knows that

big **e**lephants **c**an **a**lways **u**nderstand **s**mall **e**lephants.

moth**er**
moth

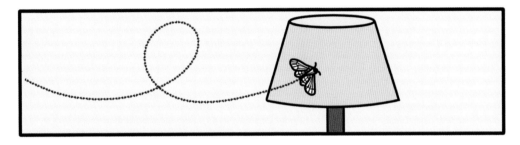

A **moth** sat on the lamp.

And made my **moth**er jump.

Noooo!

My **moth**er cried out, "Noooo!"

And swallowed the **moth** whole.

school
super children a-choo!

Super children go to school.

Secret code word is "A-choo."

If you ever hear "A-choo!,"

That's a super child at school.

you

Is it true no one can beat y**o**u in soccer?

Yep! It always kicks the ball when no one is watching. What a sporty word...

oh
oh, **h**ello!

2
Common Tricky Spelling Patterns

all (-all)
a lost lesson

The **t**all teacher in the h**all**

c**all**ed **all** players by the w**all**,

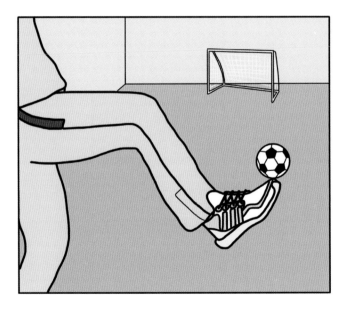

and gave them a b**all** so sm**all**,

it went up but didn't f**all**.

And that was **all**...

ate (-ate)

A d**ate** on a pl**ate**

for a pir**ate** and his m**ate**.

But who **ate** it first,

and who was too l**ate**?

ea- (-ea)
I eat my meal by the sea

Each year I eat my meal on a beach by the sea.

A healthy feast instead of beans or cheap meal deals.

I reach for wheat bread with cream spread, lean meat, and peas.

Pears and peaches—a real feast to say the least.

-ght
good hiding trees

These are **g**ood **h**iding **t**rees

at ni**ght**

and when it's li**ght**.

The tree on the ri**ght** mi**ght** look rather sli**ght**

but it's a good hiding tree all ri**ght**.

How many elves are hiding in the trees at ni**ght**?

-ould
oh, you (u) little duck

Could you cross the pond? Oh, you little duck.

Would you hurt your legs? Oh, you little duck.

Could I be your friend? Oh, you little duck.

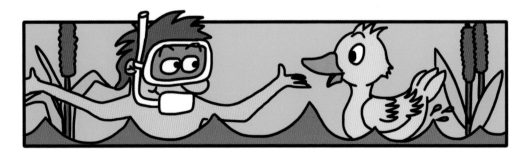

I should help you then. Oh, you lucky duck.

-ough
oh, you (u) grumpy hippo

Oh, you grumpy hippo,
enough with feeling blue.

You might be rough and tough
but you just won't pass through.

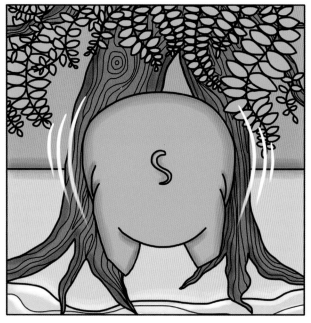

Stop pushing your hardest, don't
plough through the poor tree.

Squeeze under the low bough
and walk around it. See?

-ous
to us

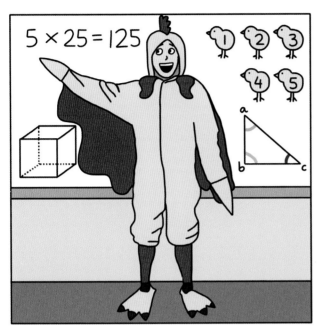

Is Mr. Wilson humor**ous**?
T**o us**, he is.

Are roads danger**ous**?
T**o us**, they are.

Did Milly look nerv**ous**?
T**o us**, she did.

Is Mrs. Morris gener**ous**?
T**o us**, she is. Very!

sure (-sure)

Would you like to find a hidden treasure? **Sure**!

Great job! Will you play again? **Sure**, Coach. My plea**sure**!

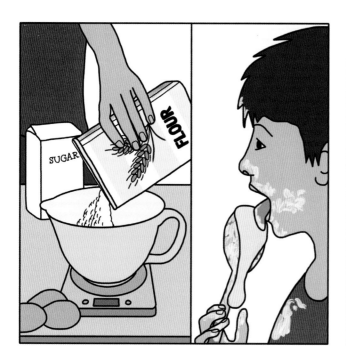

Could you help me mea**sure** flour and sugar? **Sure**!

Finally some lei**sure** time. **L**et's **e**at **i**ce cream. **Sure**.

-ture
today you (u) are (r) epic

You've drawn the best pic**ture**
and made the best sculp**ture**.

You've remembered the "e"
in temp**era**t**ure**.

You haven't frac**ture**d your knee
in soccer.

You've listened to the na**ture**
in the forest.

You've taken your little sister on an adven**ture**.

You've learned not to tor**ture** little garden crea**ture**s. Ever!

Today U R Epic!

You haven't broken your sister's building blocks struc**ture**.

You have a shining fu**ture**, my boy!

3
Number Spellings

one

only **one** elephant

two

two t**w**ins

three

th**ree** feels **f**ree
(but the first sound
is different)

four

four people in **our** family

five

five **ve**sts

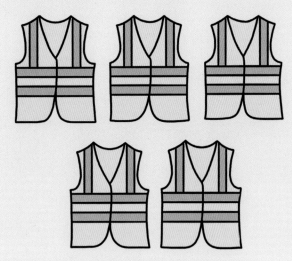

for fi**ve** children walking to school together

six

six helps to m**ix**

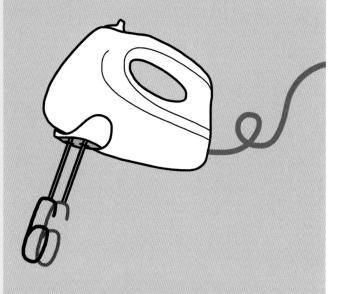

to fi**x** a yummy dessert

seven eleven

s**even** rhymes with el**even**

But have you noticed they are not **even** numbers?

eight

ei**gh**t **g**ood **h**iding **t**rees

You'll struggle to find me!

nine

nine feels fine

Sometimes it feels div**ine**!

ten

t**en** m**en**

One would do just fine
on the bathroom door, B**en**!

twelve

tw**elve elve**s

twelfth

tw**elf**th **elf**

The tw**elf**th **elf** is just
one **elf** when you spell it.

thirty

thirty looks **dirty**

Thi**rty** days without a wash.
That's a whole month, th**irty**!
Off to the bath now!

forty

forty is naughty

It has kicked off its "**u**"!

fifty

fifty **is f**unny

If only **fi**fty wasn't so w**if**ty,
it would be the funniest
stand-up comedian.

thousand

thousand grains of s**and**

To **us**, a th**ous**and feels like
a truck load of s**and**.

4
"Seeing" Words

Some words have eyes inside them.

see

seen

look

eyes

peek

peer

peep

5
"Ear" Words

And some words have ears inside them.

Every day at school, I hr and I ln.

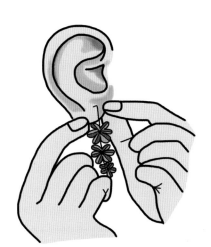 I wr my rings on my .

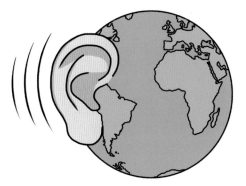 What if the rth had an and could hr us? It does. But it doesn't have a mouth to tell us to be kinder to her.

 Bob's brd is from  to .

6

Homophones and Words that "Go Together"

advise or advice?
devise or device?
Is it a snake or a cat?

Meet **S**nake, an active animal that **s**lides in a **s**erpentine motion. It **s**imply never **s**tops!

And here is **C**at, a **c**omfort **c**reature that doesn't want to be active when it doesn't have to be. **C**at is **c**omfy.

Snake and Cat have important jobs to do when it comes to spelling. One is doing a lot, the other... nothing at all.

verb
doing word

noun
non-doing word

to advise

When you advise someone, you do it actively by speaking or writing to them.

the advice

But a piece of advice (or the advice) is given to you without you having to lift your finger.

to devise

Our teacher devised a way to count all of us as we come into the classroom.

a device

The little electronic device rests in his hand every time the recess is over.

affect or effect?
action or result?

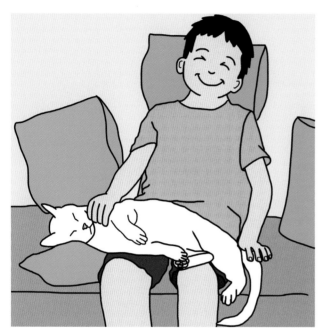

My cat's napping **a**ffected my school grades. I could never get up to do homework!

I'm sure you can help me with math, Snowflake.

Guess who's not allowed to play outside now?

One person's (or cat's) **a**ction **a**ffects the behavior of the other, which brings a r**e**sult, or **e**ffect.

Think of RAVEN

verb = **doing** word
noun = **non-doing** word

R **R**emember
A **A**ffect
V **V**erb
E **E**ffect
N **N**oun

aloud or allowed?

a
loud
orchestra
uses
drums

allowed
low

Why are **low** flying planes not allowed in urban areas? They create "noise pollution" for people and animals.

Some military planes make the ground shake!

angle or angel?

ang**le**
glue

Did you check the an**gle** before you **gl**ued the picture to the wall?

Why do an**gel**s always look beautiful?

angel
gel

They use a lot of hair **gel**. There are some rebels, though.

bear or bare?

bear
ear

Why does the **bar**tender tell feet to take off their shoes before serving them in the **bar**?

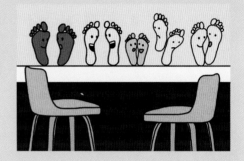

Why are my **ear**s so small?

bare
bar

Polar b**ear**s have small **ear**s to avoid losing heat. They stay warm in very cold climates.

So they can't argue they are all right!

berry or bury?

What looks like a b**e**rry but isn't?

Why do dogs b**u**ry their bones **u**nderground?

Because no one else will do it for them.

berry
cherry

A ch**e**rry, which is a fruit. B**e**rries don't have stones but have lots of seeds in their skin.

bury
underground

break or brake?

break easily

Hands up everyone who br**ea**ks things **ea**sily!

Always b**rake** when you see a **rake**!

brake
rake

cereal or serial?

real
ce**real**
corn

Cereal, such as **c**orn flakes, is made from **real c**orn.

seri**al**
seri**es**

Serial numbers follow one another in **seri**es.

Why was **s**ix afraid of **s**even?

0006	0007	0008
0009	0010	0011

Because seven ate nine.

compliment or complement?

compliment
i like

I like compliments but I blush and I don't know what to say.

"Your singing is lovely."

"Oh, no. It's really awful. I... I mean... Thank you."

complement
complete

Butter completes bread—the two complement each other.

Other matching pairs are:
- hamburgers and fries
- salt and pepper
- Batman and Robin.

Umm... Your turn!

currant or current?

currant
ant

I'm pretending I'm a currant!

This is not going to end well, is it? Get out, or you'll get eaten.

current
river

Did you know that some river currents can be turned into electricity? How exciting!

dairy or diary?

dairy
air holes

Is it really mice that make **air** holes in cheese?

Who knows? The history of d**air**y seems to be full of holes.

How do I know Gregg Heffley likes comics as much as I do?

i
am
reading

I am **r**eading *Diary of a Wimpy Kid.*

deer or dear?

deer
eer**ie**

How can d**eer** live in **eer**ie forests and yet be so timid?

Dear
ear**phones**

Let's not play hide and seek. I need to h**ear** that song again and you need untangling.

Love, Isabella

desert or dessert?

de**s**ert
sand

de**ss**ert
sweet
stuff

Why don't pirates ever get hungry on de**s**ert islands?

Because of all the **s**and which is there.

sɐɥɔᴉʍpuɐs

My favorite **s**weet **s**tuff has to have strawberries in it:
- **s**trawberry **s**hortcake
- **s**trawberry **s**ponge
- **s**trawberry **s**wirl
- **s**trawberry **s**wiss roll.

fair or **f**are?

fair
air

fare
far

May I have a **far**e that will take me **far** enough to miss the vet's today, please?

This **far**e will take you **far**!

It's not **f**air Tom was longer in the **air**!

Being suspended on a broken wheel for hours is not fun, Sid.

grate or great?

grate
rat

What do **gr**a**t**ers and **rat**s have in common?

They both like cheese.

great
eat

It's gr**eat** to **eat** your favorite food!

Eat,
not play
with
your
food,
Mario.

heal or heel?

heal
alright

Is your finger he**al**ing **al**right?

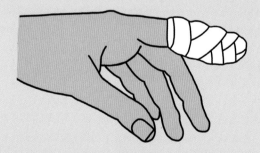

Hard to tell. I haven't had my game console in my hands since Friday.

heel
elegant

Mom has two **ele**gant heels.

One foot looks better in high heel shoes, the other in low ones. Does she not limp?
Yes, she does, but **ele**gantly.

lose or loose?

lose

Mom complains my oldest brother is not good with money:

"If money could talk, his would only ever say 'Goodbye'..."

Why are Betty's two front teeth loose?
She's English and she says "candy floss" for "cotton candy." Betty thought candy floss and dental floss were the same thing! But there is something that keeps her loose teeth together. It's toothpaste.

mail or male?

snail
mail

male
Alex

Did you know that "snail mail" actually exists in the real world?

Letters that we drop in a mail box are called snail mail.

Some names are both male and female.
Take Alex. When you hear about a baby called Alex, you don't know if it's a boy or a girl. Can you think of other names that can be both male and female?

meat or meet?

meat
eat

meet
greet

I like to **eat** meat.

Grrrrr!

But I don't like to m**eet** and gr**eet**!

new or knew?

What do you call a brand **new** t-shirt?

never
ever
worn

What do you call a bad day at the CNN?
Nothing **n**ew to report.

knew
kicked

I **k**icked myself because I **k**new the answer.

72

not or knot?

What do these DO NOT signs mean?

Clockwise: do not enter; do not use phone; do not feed birds; do not run; do not touch.

knot

What's a pretzel?

Bread in a knot.

one or won?

only
one
on earth

Isn't it amazing there is only one of you on earth?

Can you win it?

"One" or "won"?
If you can win it,
it has a "w" in it.

pair or pear?

pair
air

pear
eat

This p**air** of sneakers makes me fly in the **air**!

When I **eat** a p**ear**, I feel full because it has fiber.
I then don't crave sugary snacks. I love to **eat** p**ear**s!

pea**ce** or pie**ce**?

peace
pea

pie**ce**
pie

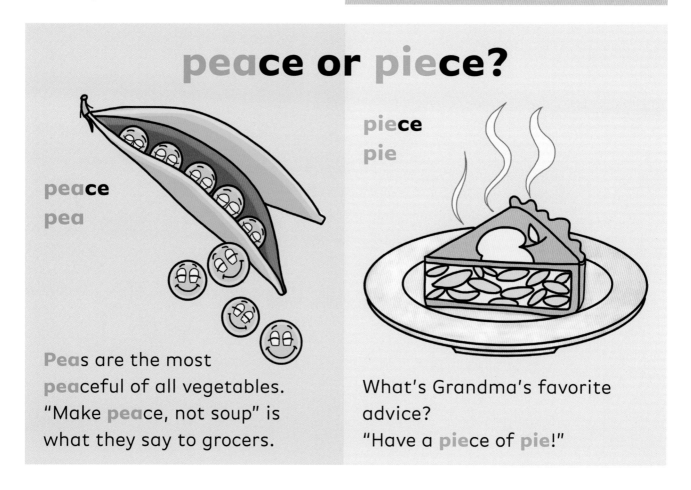

Peas are the most **pea**ceful of all vegetables. "Make **pea**ce, not soup" is what they say to grocers.

What's Grandma's favorite advice?
"Have a pie**ce** of **pie**!"

peek or peak?

peek

"No peeking," said Mom just as Peter peeked into the oven to see what was cooking.

"Not eels in leeks again!"

"Why did Peter flee so fast before dinner?" wondered Mom.

peak A

Some letters look like things in the real world.

The letter **A** looks like a ladder, angle, alligator's mouth, duck's beak, and a peak!

plane or plain?

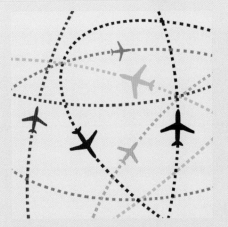

plane lane

Do planes use lanes? Yes, they follow invisible spots called coordinates. They don't fly in straight lines but from one spot to another.

plain in white

The bride looked lovely, but Ben thought he looked plain in white. Cheer up, Ben. Stop looking down in the mouth. It's a wedding!

see or sea?

I'm a ninja!
No, you're not, Dad.
Ha! Did you **see** me do that?
Do what?
Exactly!

sea
animals

Can you draw four other se**a a**nimals?		

seen or scene?

seen

How do you know carrots are good for you?

How?

Have you s**ee**n a rabbit wearing glasses?

crime
scene
central

Why did Mr. Potato call the **C**rime **S**c**e**n**e** **C**e**n**tral line?

His wife wasn't in the same room when he saw a neighbor try ketchup on fries.

some or sum?

some money

Here's some money, Tom. Just remember I'm not a bank and money doesn't grow on trees.

That's not true. Banks have branches!

sum of numbers

$$2+7=9$$

Why are you doing your math on the floor, Lucia?

The teacher told us not to use tables.

To sum it up, numbers are no fun for Lucia.

son or sun?

son boy

Who's Mommy's little boy?

sun fun

We run and run, having fun in the sun. Summer has begun!

stationary or stationery?

Ahoy, M**a**tey.
Ye want t'be station**a**ry?
Anchor the ship then, **a**rrrr.

We asked a hundred people to name an item of station**e**ry.

⊠ ⊠ ⊠ ⊠ ⊠ ⊠ ⊠ ⊠ ⊠ ⊠
⊠ ⊠ ⊠ ⊠ ⊠ ⊠ ⊠ ⊠ ⊠ ⊠
⊠ ⊠ ⊠ ⊠ ⊠ ⊠ ⊠ ⊠ ⊠ ⊠
⊠ ⊠ ⊠ ⊠ ⊠ ⊠ ⊠ ⊠ ⊠ ⊠
⊠ ⊠ ⊠ ⊠ ⊠ ⊠ ⊠ ⊠ ⊠ ⊠
⊠ ⊠ ⊠ ⊠ ⊠ ⊠ ⊠ ⊠ ⊠ ⊠
⊠ ⊠ ⊠ ⊠ ⊠ ⊠ ⊠ ⊠ ⊠ ⊠
⊠ ⊠ ⊠ ⊠ ⊠ ⊠ ⊠ ⊠ ⊠ ⊠
⊠ ⊠ ⊠ ⊠ ⊠ ⊠ ⊠ ⊠ ⊠ ⊠
⊠ ⊠ ⊠ ⊠ ⊠ ⊠ ⊠ ⊠ ⊠ ✎

Ninety-nine said **e**nvelope.

thr**ew** or thr**ough**?

thr**ew**
ew!

Mom thr**ew** away Javier's old sneakers.
"**Ew**!" was all she said.

Can hippos pass thr**ough** obstacles without pl**ough**ing them down?

oh
u (you)
grumpy
hippo

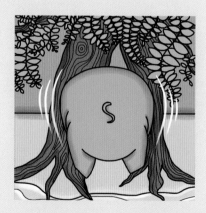

Not if they are grumpy! Also see page 40.

there or their?

there
here

Start with **here**.
If it's not **here**,
it's over t**here**.

Whe**re**?
Over t**here**.

their
gi**r**ls
di**r**t
sh**ir**ts
sk**ir**ts

The **g**i**r**ls got **d**i**r**t on the**ir** sh**ir**ts and sk**ir**ts.

I'd like to be in the**ir** school!

or they're?

Think paper clip,
think apostrophe.

they **a**re

they│re

┃ = ,

they're means **they are**

too or two?

too
cool

Can anyone be t**oo** c**oo**l?
This guy can.

When he
walks by,
people get
chills and
his fans get
brain freeze!

two
twins

There can only be **tw**o **tw**ins.
One, **tw**o. **Tw**o **tw**irling and
twisting **tw**ins.

wait or weight?

w**A**it
4
it

I'm watching my sister take
a selfie.

Wait for it... (W**A**it **4** it...)

What's the wei**gh**t of **g**ood
hiding **t**rees?

good
hiding
trees

Heavy. Twelve elves are hiding
in them!

weather or whether?

weather
sea

What's the weather at sea like today?

The weather at sea is not looking good. A storm is on its way.

whether
he

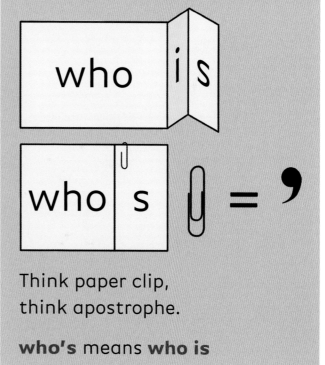

Whether he wanted to or not, he had to made a decision...

whose or who's?

whose
nose

Whose nose is the odd one out?

who is

who s ⊘ = '

Think paper clip, think apostrophe.

who's means **who is**

witch or which?

wit
w**itch**
itch

Why do **wit**ches
cackle?
Because they
are **wit**ty.

Why do w**itch**es ride on
broomsticks?
Because they have **itch**y feet.

wh

wh**o?**
wh**at?**
wh**ere?**
wh**en?**
wh**y?**
wh**ich?**

Which is yet another question
that starts with "**wh**."

your or you're?

your = you®

If something belongs to
someone, you will say to them,
"This is you**r** _____."

The "**r**" at the end of "you**r**" is
there just like the trademark
sign ® is placed after a
name that belongs to an
organization. ® says: "This
brand is ours. It belongs to us."

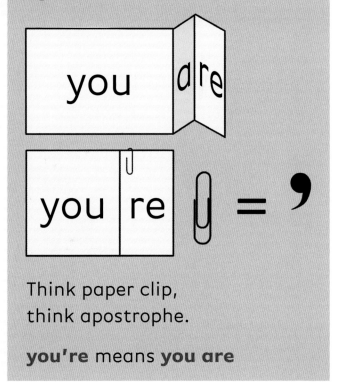

Think paper clip,
think apostrophe.

you're means **you are**

7
Letter Sandwiches

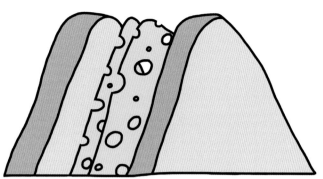

interest

May I int**ere**st you in sandwich making?

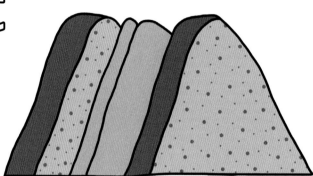

every

Every sandwich needs a filling.

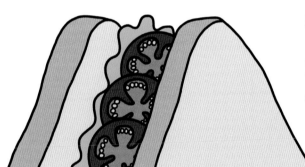

follow

Follow your nose and see what you can find in the refrigerator.

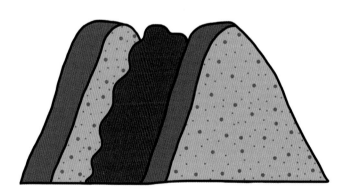

even

Does the jelly look **eve**n on each side?

a w a y

Don't throw any cheese **awa**y.
Put an extra slice in.

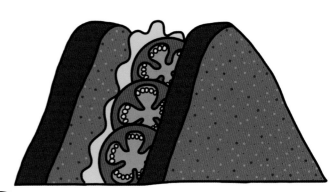

diff**ere**nt

Why not make your sandwich diff**ere**nt?
Use whole-wheat bread instead.

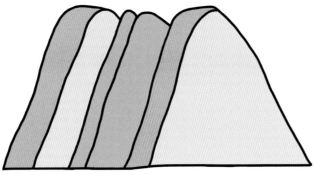

b **ette** r

Are two slices of ham
b**ette**r than one?

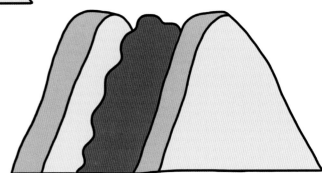

def **i** n **i** te

Now, this sandwich is a def**ini**te winner!

8

High- and Medium-Frequency Words, Including Spelling Exceptions

actu**ally**

Ally has **act**ed like she's on my side.

Actu**ally**, **Ally** is my **ally**! **Act**-u-**ally**!

again

again
Britain
rain

What happens in Brit**ain** ag**ain** and ag**ain**?

R**ain**.

athlete

exactly
ten
events

A decathlon athl**ete** has to compete in **e**xactly **t**en **e**vents.

balloon

Balloons are **ball**-shaped **loon**y inflatables. Did you know they are scared of just one type of music?

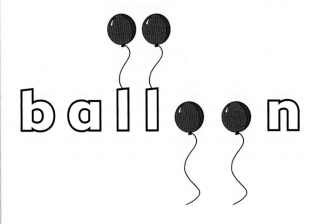

Pop music!

beautiful

big
ears
aren't
ugly

Big **e**ars **a**ren't **u**gly. They are **beau**tiful.

Always **be a** beautiful girl inside and out.

bicycle

uncle
bi**cycle**
icy

Don't ride your b**icy**cle when it's **icy**.

Yes, Un**cle Cle**o...

blue

What should you do when you see a blu**e e**lephant?

Cheer him up!

build

You and **I** (**ui**) will build a house.

After you've done your homework, boys.

Oh, Moooom!

busy

busy
bus

The **bus** was so **bus**y,
I finally had a chance to be
a stuntman!

care/scared

are
c**are**
s**c**are**d**

I know you **are** **s**c**are**d, Bella.
I'll be very **c**are**ful listening to
your heart. I'll take good **c**are
of you.

church

ch   ur   ch

Put "ch" on the left
and "ch" on the right,
and you are (**ur**) in the middle.

competition

competition
pet

When **Pet**al has won again,
her owner **Pet**unia declared:
"The only real com**pet**ition is
a **pet** com**pet**ition."

daughter

dear
Alice
u (you)
got
hairy
toes

We all have hairy toes but the hair is so small we can't see it.

Dear Mom, so do you! Alice

de**sign**

design
signature

A good de**sign**er always puts a **sign**ature on their de**sign**s.

down

Down! Low on the floor.

down
low

Owen trained his **ow**ner to smile every time he stayed l**ow**.

easy

egg
and
spoon

"The **egg** **a**nd **s**poon race is so **eas**y," said James a moment before he was disqualified for using both hands.

family

father
and
mother
i
love
you

Mom and Dad loved Ben's **family** picture.

first/bird/birthday

first
bird
birthday

I got my **fi**rst **bi**rd on my **bi**rthday. Her singing **ir**ritated the neighbors, but the**ir** cat was a real fan!

fascinating

fa**sc**inating
sleeping
cats

Sleeping **c**ats are fa**sc**inating.

But don't touch Pebbles' nose. Cats lose appetite if their sense of smell is upset.

fasten

fasten
going **fast**

Fasten your seatbelt, Snuggles. We are going **fast**!

friend

i
fri**end**
end

"You're tickling me, buddy. **I**, till the **end**, will be your fr**i****end**!"

girl

"That **g**irl **is** **r**eally **l**ovely," thought Jake...

girl
is
really
lovely

until he saw her pick her nose at recess.

innocent

in
no
cent**ury**

In **no** **cent**ury was crime treated as something **innocent**.

know/knight/knee

know
knight
knock
knee

Do you **kn**ow why **kn**ights never look scared even when they tremble with fear?

They **kn**ock their **kn**ees with silent "**k**"s!

laugh

Buddy's joke was so good Adam had to enter him in a pet talent competition.

laugh
and
u (you)
get
happy

lightning

There is no "e" in ligh**tn**ing. Just see what happened to it!

ligh**t**ning

listen

lis**ten**

ten songs

On Saturday, Joe lis**ten**s to **ten** songs from the Top **Ten** Chart.

little

teeny tiny little eggs

What do you think might have happened in the bird's nest?

necessary

It's necessary for Billy to put on one collar (**c**) and two socks (**ss**) when he gets ready for school.

_1 collar

_2 socks

neighbor

neighbor
giant
honey
bear

Cara! Our nei**gh**bor is a **g**iant **h**oney **b**ear!

notice

ice
notice
police

**POLICE
NOTICE**

Are you ready for ice on the roads? Slow down and expect delays. Do not drive unless it is necessary.

Pol**ice** issued a not**ice** about **ice** on the road.

now

There's no better time than **n**ow—unless it's the time to get up.

occasionally

Occasionally, Billy represents his school in sports events. He puts on an extra shirt—he now has two collars (**cc**) but only one sock (**s**).

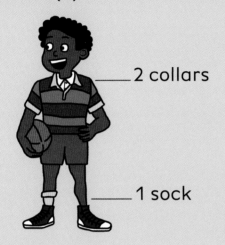

——— 2 collars

——— 1 sock

ocean

only
cats'
eyes
are
narrow

Did you know? Sea otters are called "the cats of the **ocean**." They are cute, playful, and enjoy wrapping up in seaweed when taking long naps.

often

out of ten

I **often** score my pranks out **of ten**.

Creeping up on my brother with cymbals is **ten** out of **ten**! Even if I'm not allowed to do it more **often**...

out

O U Trouble!

Pebbles gave no comment...

pe**o**ple

pe**o**ple

People live on the Earth and the round planet (**o**) lives in the spelling of the word "pe**o**ple."

pre**sent**

sent
pre**sent**

When she **sent** the pre**sent**, the blue mailbox couldn't open its mouth wide enough to keep the ribbon and bow neat.

That's why pre**sent**s are best **sent** from the post office.

qu**een**

queen + **u**mbrella
q + u

You will never see the **q**ueen without her **u**mbrella.

When you write a "**q**," always follow it with a "**u**."

rhythm

rhythm
helps
your
two
hips
move

How do you tell if a tissue has **rhythm**?
You put a little boogie in it.

shoulder

shoulder
should

Well done, Zhang Wei! You **should** pat yourself on the **should**er.

Also see page 39.

sign

sign
signal

A **sign** is a kind of **sign**al that tells us what to do.

surprise

burp
surprise
rise

Arjun **burp**ed all night. It will be a **surp**rise if we see him **rise** early.

weird

weird
we
a**we**some

Yes, **we** are **we**ird.
Yes, **we** are a**we**some!

wood/would

You won't confuse w**oo**d for w**ou**ld when you imagine two w**oo**d logs inside the word. Think w**oo**d, think logs.

Think w**ou**ld, think a little duck (see page 39).

young

young
you

You are young...

"**You** are so **you**ng, child..." thought Grandad.

Index

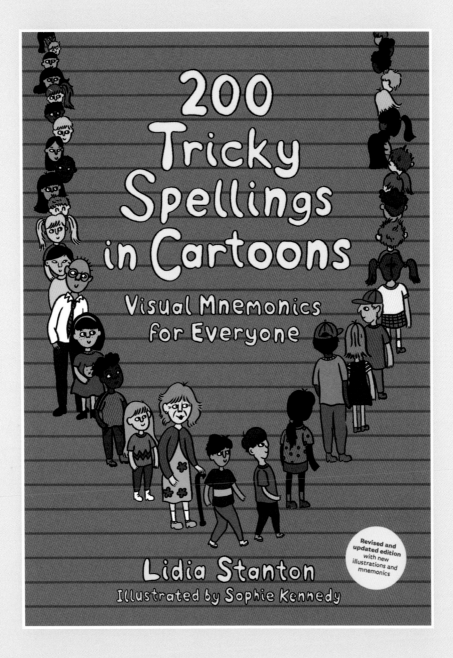

A visual guide to learning 200 of the trickiest spellings, with memorable mnemonics, cartoons, and storylines. Lidia Stanton's cartoons provide visual hints and tricks to help kids who think or learn differently to make sense of the most confusing spellings, including homophones and exceptions.

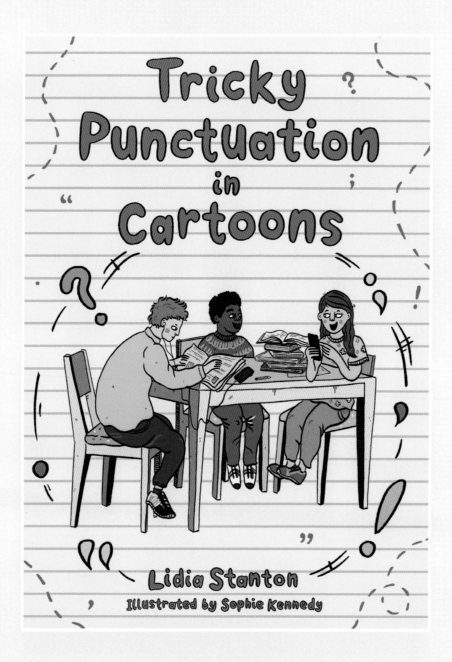

This illustrated punctuation workbook supports students with dyslexia, ADHD, or other learning difficulties to develop punctuation skills via inquiry-based learning. The book encourages students to engage in active learning to make their own connections about tricky punctuation. It provides a wealth of fun ways to remember the required rules.

Other JKP Titles

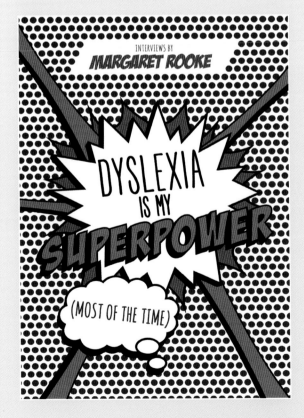

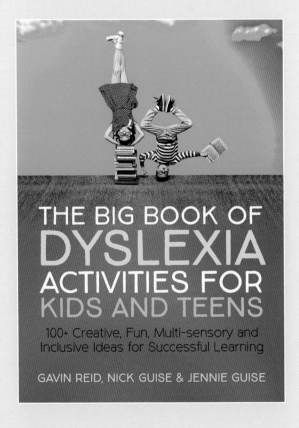

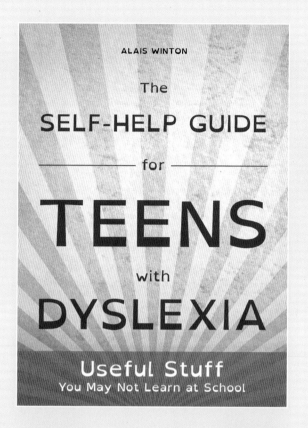

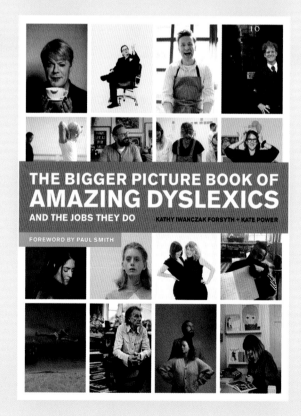